A Church Lacking
Book 2

Preface:

In the first book in this series, we saw many things the church is lacking today. However, it is not the church that is to be blamed. It is us personally. If we can apply a few disciplines to our life on a personal level, we will be able to see the effect trickle over into the church. In this book I want us to look at 4 different areas. Confidence, dependance, focused and to be ready. A church that has put their confidence in the Lord, a church that is dependent on the Lord, a church that is focused upon the Lord and a church that is ready for the return of the Lord is a church that will not be lacking. Let us pick up where we left off in the previous book.

This book is dedicated to those churches that do not want to just come in and meet for services once a week, but for those who want to be a force in the Kingdom of God.

Chapter 1
A Church Dependent

Hebrews 12:18-29

It's pretty easy to get a group of people into an argument. It's not talking about politics . . . it's about asking their opinions. It's to ask the question . . . "What or who is the greatest?"

So, let's get the debate going . . .
What's the greatest car ever made?
Who's the greatest president ever?
Who's the greatest basketball player of all time?
Who's the greatest composer?
What's the greatest movie of all time?
What's the greatest Christian song?

These are pretty simple questions, but they can get a few people wound up because others are disagreeing with their opinion about who or what is the greatest. We can get pretty passionate about our opinions.

Raising our voices, making our points, repeating our points.

One thing I think we can all agree on is Jesus is the GREATEST! That's really one of the points the author of Hebrews has been making all along. When Jesus is compared to the competition, the answer is always Jesus! Jesus is the greatest.

The writer demonstrated earlier in this book that,

Jesus is greater than Angels (1:4-2:18)
Jesus is greater than Moses (3:1-6)

Jesus is greater than Aaron (4:14 to 5:10)
Jesus is greater than Melchizedek (7:1-17)

I want you to see in this chapter how Jesus is greater than the law.

To better understand this, we need to better know what the LAW is. The law is defined by the Hebrew word TORAH. The Torah for Jewish people is comprised of the first 5 books of the Bible in the Old Testament. Those would be

Genesis Exodus Leviticus Numbers Deuteronomy

The word Torah means "The Law!" For the Jewish people they held onto the law. That's how they lived their lives. Everything was about the law. They would not ask 'do you know God?' But 'are you following the law?' That's what was most important for them.

In fact, in the first 5 books of the Bible there are 613 laws or commandments. 365 are thou shalt not, while 248 state "thou shall". That's a lot to remember and not mess up. The most well-known laws are the 10 commandments, found in Exodus 20.

The point of this final section of Hebrews 12 is that we are no longer under the law, but we are under grace, through Jesus Christ. And being under grace is so much greater than being under the law!

So, let's look at Hebrews 12:18-21

Hebrews 12:18-21

For ye are not come unto the mount that might be touched, and that burned with fire, nor unto blackness, and darkness, and tempest, And the sound of a trumpet, and the voice of words; which voice they that heard intreated that the word should not be spoken to them any more: (For they could not endure that which was commanded, And if so much as a beast touch the mountain, it shall be stoned, or thrust through with a dart: And so terrible was the sight, that Moses said, I exceedingly fear and quake:)

The writer wants the people to look back to the scene in Exodus 19:16 and 18 in which we can paint a vivid picture of what was happening on Mt. Sinai. Moses was up on the mountain receiving the 10 Commandments from God, and this what the people are experiencing while Moses is up the mountain.

Exodus 19:16-19
And it came to pass on the third day in the morning, that there were thunders and lightnings, and a thick cloud upon the mount, and the voice of the trumpet exceeding loud; so that all the people that was in the camp trembled. And Moses brought forth the people out of the camp to meet with God; and they stood at the nether part of the mount. And mount Sinai was altogether on a smoke, because the Lord descended upon it in fire: and the smoke thereof ascended as the smoke of a furnace, and the whole mount quaked greatly. And when the voice of the trumpet sounded long, and waxed louder and louder, Moses spake, and God answered him by a voice.

It's a tense situation.
There's drama.

The mountain is dark, there's smoke, the mountain is shaking.
And the people are freaking out. They could not approach God on the mountain, except for Moses. Not even a beast was allowed to come near the mountain.
It's like the put a police line around the mountain so that nobody would approach it and go too far. If a person or an animal got too close, they would certainly die. Hebrews also tells us that Moses was even trembling. That's how terrifying this scene is. And that is the exact image the writer wants us to understand.

Now he does a compare and contrast of Mount Sinai with Mount Zion.

He's doing what we might try to do if we were to try and describe a zebra to a child who has never seen a zebra.

The child asks, "What is a zebra?"

We might say, "A zebra is an animal, picture what a horse looks like, but not quite as big as a horse. It also has stripes mostly going up and down on it whole body.
The stripes are like the stripes of a tiger, but they are not black and orange, they are black and white.

We end up using comparison and contrast to explain what a zebra looks like. As long as the child knows what a tiger and horse look like, he or she will be able to get a good idea about what a zebra looks like.

In a similar way the writer in Hebrews compares and Judaism and Christianity - - -

The Old Covenant and the New Covenant.

He does it by using 2 pictures of mountains:

Mount Sinai (physical mountain).

Mount Zion (spiritual mountain).

So, as we move forward, the writer of Hebrews tells us:

Hebrews 12:22-24
But ye are come unto mount Sion, and unto the city of the living God, the heavenly Jerusalem, and to an innumerable company of angels, To the general assembly and church of the firstborn, which are written in heaven, and to God the Judge of all, and to the spirits of just men made perfect, And to Jesus the mediator of the new covenant, and to the blood of sprinkling, that speaketh better things than that of Abel.

Can you see the difference in tone and attitude in these verses compared to what the first verses sounded like?

The writer is talking about the living God,
heavenly Jerusalem,
innumerable angels in festal gatherings,
spirits of the righteous made perfect,
God the judge,
Jesus, the mediator of a new covenant.

This sounds so much better than mountains and people trembling.

Sinai was a place of fear, trembling, horror; as the people were confronted with the Law, commandments, judgement, and condemnation.

Zion is a picture of grace, forgiveness, atonement, and salvation.

Sinai was forbidding and terrifying,

Zion is inviting and gracious;

Sinai was closed to all. You could not approach the mountain or you'd die. You can even see today when you study the archeology of that place that there was a border set up to keep you from the mountain.

Zion is open to all because Jesus Christ has met the terms of Sinai and will stand in the place of anyone who places their faith in Him.

So, there is no need to fear or tremble regarding our judgment, because Jesus has paid the price for you and I.

The world's vision of God in that day was based upon the booming voice of God that sounded like 100's of trumpet blasts. A sound that would strike fear and dread into the hearts of the people. It was based on the smoke, fire and darkness of the cloud that sat upon the mountain symbolizing God's power and that fact that He hid His face from people or they would be instantly destroyed.

When God would speak to the people, they would beg Moses to tell God to stop. They simply could not endure His power; and they couldn't understand God's mercy and grace; and had no assurance in their hearts of being treated as a son or daughter of God. They felt more like subjects of God than children of God.

Ah, but now we are invited to Zion, not Sinai. Though faith in Christ we can get a vision of God that no one could have dreamed of in the Old Testament. Through faith the way is now opened so we could come before the very presence of God, right into the very Throne Room of God, which is far greater than going into the Holy of Holies. We don't approach God through the Mercy Seat upon the Ark of the Covenant with the blood of a lamb; that we looked at earlier in Hebrews, but we approach the God of Mercy through the blood of Jesus.

Where once there was lightning, thunder, fire and trumpets; now there is praise, worship and glorifying God. Where once there was a warning to not touch God's mountain for fear of death; now there is an open invitation to come right up on the mountain and commune with God one on one.

We are called to eat with Him, as He eats with us. What an amazing, powerful and glorious difference!

We no longer approach God begging for mercy. For once we accept Jesus as Lord and Savior, the door is now opened into a new life, eternal life on earth and in the future.
We can approach God as His beloved, holy and dear children. We are no longer condemned and doomed. We are now viewed as righteous, not because of what we've done, but because of what Christ did for us.

As we move to the end, the writer concludes with words of warning and hope

Hebrews 12:25-27
See that ye refuse not him that speaketh. For if they escaped not who refused him that spake on earth, much more shall not we escape, if we turn away from him that speaketh from heaven: Whose voice then shook the earth: but now he hath promised, saying, Yet once more I shake not the earth only, but also heaven. And this word, Yet once more, signifieth the removing of those things that are shaken, as of things that are made, that those things which cannot be shaken may remain.

The point the writer is trying to make is this . . .

Because the new covenant is superior, Christ is calling for a response from the people. He warned us while on earth, that the people need to make Christ Jesus Lord of their life. Part of this is a reference to the Jewish people from the exodus but that warning extends to all people.

We are not to reject the call of Christ. Ultimately there is the warning from verse 26 that the earth and the heavens will be shaken. This is not about people losing their salvation once they're in heaven, it's about the created order of things. That's why the writer spoke about things that are made in verse 27.

As a result, the writer says in the final verses,

Hebrews 12:28-29
Wherefore we receiving a kingdom which cannot be moved, let us have grace, whereby we may serve God

acceptably with reverence and godly fear: For our God is a consuming fire.

Part of the beauty and power of God is the fact that we receive a kingdom which cannot be shaken!

Isn't that great news!
Glory!!!!
That's powerful news folks.
Nothing can defeat our God!
Nothing can make our God nervous and afraid!
God doesn't tremble and shake!
Because God is that solid rock and because of that we are to offer to God acceptable worship with reverence and awe.

We should come into the building every Sunday, no matter if it's been a good or bad week, with a sense of expectation. We should expect to meet the risen Christ. So, we come prepared and ready to worship in a manner which is honoring to God. We do it with reverence and awe.

Go all the way back to the beginning of this message . . . if you could meet the greatest person ever . . . wouldn't you get prepared, ready, have a set of questions to ask? In the same way, when you come into this building, you should come here prepared and ready to meet the King of kings and Lord of lords.

So, the point is this, if you are still living life on the basis of the old covenant, that old law which so easily traps us and condemns us, then let's find a way to help you move into worshiping the God of grace, not the God of the law. You can't do it through the law. The law is about you.

Depending on you. Quit depending on you and start depending on Jesus Christ.

Admit your need. Proclaim it to God that you need Him.

Let me end with a picture of grace for you . . .

In an old Dennis the Menace cartoon, Dennis and his little friend Joey are leaving Mrs. Wilson's house, their hands are full of cookies.

Joey says to Dennis, "I wonder what we did to deserve this."

Dennis answers, "Look, Joey. Mrs. Wilson gives us cookies not because we're nice, but because she's nice."

That cartoon is a simple picture of grace.

God saved us …not because we're nice and deserved it;

But because He created us in His image and He loves us!

Church it is time to become less self-dependent and more God dependent. God has made a way for you today. Will you call upon Him, Lord I can't but you can. I am depending on you.

Chapter 2
A Church Confident

Hebrews 13:1-6

Have you ever been in a situation where you wonder
'what's the right thing to do in this situation?'
You wonder about it, but most of the time even though we
know what the right thing is to do, we don't do it. So many
times, we avoid doing the right thing because doing the
right thing is often not the popular thing and is usually
more difficult than doing nothing.

Think about a kid in your school who is getting bullied by
that popular person.
It happens in front of other students and even in front of
teachers who do nothing about it. It aggravates you and
you know the person being bullied feels horrible.
But what do you do? Most everyone in class is laughing.
What's the right thing to do? You know what it is, but it's
not always easy to do. Because that is not the popular or
even the Politically Correct thing to do.

This may also be true in the workplace, where there may
even be more risk to be taken, like losing your job or
career or the promotion you wanted.

We can go down this track for so many other areas in life.
And in a few minutes, we will.

Let's see what the writer is calling for us to do and not to
do, as we seek to become more like Jesus. He wrote:

Hebrews 13:1-6

Let brotherly love continue. Be not forgetful to entertain strangers: for thereby some have entertained angels unawares. Remember them that are in bonds, as bound with them; and them which suffer adversity, as being yourselves also in the body. Marriage is honourable in all, and the bed undefiled: but whoremongers and adulterers God will judge. Let your conversation be without covetousness; and be content with such things as ye have: for he hath said, I will never leave thee, nor forsake thee. So that we may boldly say, The Lord is my helper, and I will not fear what man shall do unto me.

The writer is leading us to a place where we can state with confidence . . . The Lord is my helper, I will not fear, for what can any person do to me?

That's a great statement made with confidence
I want you to notice this statement can only be made by having their confidence in Jesus Christ. Look what the writer is saying in verse 5.

Hebrews 13:5
I will never leave you nor forsake you.

How many times have you had to question if this is really true or not? Sometimes situations and circumstances in life have led us to question, GOD ARE YOU REALLY NOT GOING TO LEAVE ME?

You're really not going to forsake me, are you? Because the way my life is going right now, it sure doesn't feel like you're there!!

Have you ever felt that way? I have! I've doubted, I've questioned, I've asked. It's not a sin to do that. It's actually part of our journey to growing deeper in Christ.

We have all this statement made may times. God has promised He will never leave you. I've said it often. I believe it! But sometimes life bites us and we hurt and we question in the midst of that hurt. It's normal, it's natural, it's OK to question. We just can't get stuck there. That's the key!!

We can't let that doubt hold us,

We can't stay in that doubt for in doing so we are doubting the very Word of God.

God has promised all followers of Christ that He Will do what?

He will Never leave you ... and ... He Will Never forsake you.

God stated this promise to the nation of Israel in Moses final message to the people, in Deuteronomy 31:6 and 8, Moses told the people, 'Don't be afraid, be courageous, God will not leave you or forsake you.'

Deuteronomy 31:6
Be strong and of a good courage, fear not, nor be afraid of them: for the Lord thy God, he it is that doth go with thee; he will not fail thee, nor forsake thee.

Deuteronomy 31:8
And the Lord, he it is that doth go before thee; he will be with thee, he will not fail thee, neither forsake thee: fear not, neither be dismayed.

As Joshua was about to lead the people into the promised land, God spoke these words to Joshua - - reminding him 3 times to be strong and courageous and that God would never leave him or forsake him.
Finally, God commanded Joshua:

Joshua 1:9
Have not I commanded thee? Be strong and of a good courage; be not afraid, neither be thou dismayed: for the Lord thy God is with thee whithersoever thou goest.

That is a great promise and it's the same promise God makes to you and I. God's people were repeatedly assured, that God would not leave them nor forsake them.

And Now, God reminds us, He promises us, He will never leave you, nor forsake us! This doesn't mean life will be easy, it means God will be with you through the good and the not so good.
It means through the ups and downs, that God will be with us.
It means through the thick and thin, He will never forsake us.
It means in sickness and in health, He will never forsake us.
No matter what the world may bring against us, the Lord has promised not to forsake us.
No matter what the devil tries to throw at us, the Lord has promised that He will never forsake us or abandon us.
No matter how many challenges come we are promised that the Lord will never forsake us.

Bad things will happen, but when we know the Lord is with us, we can be filled with great courage in the midst of our storms because He promised that He will never leave us or forsake us.

Now, to help you believe in what I'm telling you, I want to give you the literal Greek translation of this passage. Because as good as our translations are, we've made this verse too easy to read.

This passage says, *I will not leave you or forsake you*, but the actual literal translation is more definite about what God will do for us. Literally it should read this way.

He Himself has said never not you will I leave nor never not you will I forsake.

In the Greek language, as well as in English, the more negatives there are in a sentence . . . the more definite that statement is.

In scripture you will find 25 times Jesus says verily, verily. In those scripture the Lord is saying listen, listen, pay attention.

The writer of Hebrews is saying the same thing here.
The writer wants us to really believe God is not going to leave us.
He's not going to forsake us.
He's not going to abandon and He's not going to desert us.

So, with that in mind, hold onto these great words from Hebrews, and now let's take a quick look at the first verses of Hebrews 13. We are told to

Hebrews 13:1
Let brotherly love continue.

There is a point the writer is making in this verse. He is telling us we need to continue to love one another. In other words, you've already been doing it. You've already been loving one another. Keep doing it. Don't stop loving one another. Let the world see the power of Christian fellowship and love. Let them see how we care about one another, not how we beat one another up.

Sometimes we have a distorted view of how we love one another. Because often times we love only those we want to love.

Ever been there! "Oh, I don't like him or I don't like her, so, I'm not going to help them."

They don't look like I do,
They don't talk like I do.
They don't dress like I do.
They are not the same color I am.
The list goes on and on.
Even Christ followers do that! We don't always love one another. Sometimes we are too grumpy, too distracted, and too self-centered. Whatever the excuse, they are all excuses.

Do we see one another as brothers and sisters in Christ? As people we want to help, or people we want to be critical of? Do we love one another as brothers and sisters in Christ?

And the call to love one another is based on the fact that God will never, never leave us nor forsake us. So, look at one another and find a reason to love them, after all, they are your brothers and sisters in Christ.

God will never cease to love you and if you have the Spirit of Jesus Christ living in you then you should love one another.

John 13:35
By this shall all men know that ye are my disciples, if ye have love one to another.

Next we are told to do is something really interesting . . .

Hebrews 13:2
Be not forgetful to entertain strangers: for thereby some have entertained angels unawares.

We tend to think of hospitality as inviting someone over for supper. But, this verse in reality continues the theme of loving others. Showing hospitality to strangers.

This includes at church; help that person you don't know to feel welcomed. Be welcoming.

There is a difference in the gift of hospitality and being hospitable.

The gift of hospitality is the gift of serving others. It is a gift that is mentioned in scripture but to be hospitable is to be welcoming. To be friendly, to be someone that people want to be around.

The goal in being hospitable is to be welcoming. It's to help someone feel welcome in your presence.

We should be doing that at church, at work, at school. Wherever we go. In doing so we are demonstrating the presence of Jesus Christ's in our lives? It's about showing kindness, compassion, patience to others. It's offering an encouraging word.

It may mean we need to help someone in a different way. Maybe it's giving someone food, or clothes, or money. Maybe it's serving more.
You never know who that stranger is who you encounter. Yet, in the world we live in, we need to have common sense and be safe at the same time.
We never know the difference we can make in a person's life because we befriended them with kindness and compassion. That's the deeper point of this verse.

We continue with the theme of compassion

Hebrews 13:3
Remember them that are in bonds, as bound with them; and them which suffer adversity, as being yourselves also in the body.

What is the writer saying?

Remember those who are in prison, as though in prison with them, and those who are mistreated, since you also are in the body.

We know the writer here was talking about a physical prison. These Christians of this time period were being imprisoned for their faith.
They were having their lands taken away.
They were having their children taken away.

They were having their finances taken away.
The writer is saying to put yourself in their shoes. Don't look down on them, but imagine that was you.
Friend there is more prisons than just a physical prison. There are mental prisons, emotional prisons. There are spiritual prisons, there are prisons of sickness.

The writer is telling us imagine yourself in the position of those who are suffering.
He is saying put yourself in their shoes.

Not only are we to show compassion, but we add empathy. It means "understanding and entering into another person's feelings." When you practice empathy, you can't help but practice compassion.

Put yourself in the place of others. Whether at work, home, school wherever you are.
Consider those who are bullied,
Consider those who feel unloved,
Consider those who are all alone,
Consider those who are struggling,
Consider those who are hurting.
Put yourself in their shoes.
I heard a story one time about, a man who complained because he had no shoes, until he met a man who had not feet to use.

Sometimes we can get so focused upon ourselves and our own problems that we lose sight of those around us.
Most of the time our world doesn't see the Christian as a compassionate person. They see us as judgmental. They see us as having a better than thou attitude.

They see us as holier-than-thou. They see as a member of a private and exclusive club. The world needs to see us is as a people of compassion. That can only happen when we make it a habit to practice compassion.

Next, the writer moves onto the topic of being content. In verse 4, he tells us:

Hebrews 13:4
Marriage is honourable in all, and the bed undefiled: but whoremongers and adulterers God will judge.

This was a radical thing to say back in the first century. To honor your marriage and not commit adultery definitely made your faith show back then.

We are to honor our marriages and be faithful.
Do we honor our spouses?
Do we show respect, value and cherish our spouse?
Do we treat one another with kindness, humility, and grace? Do our actions loudly proclaim - - "I love you!"

Because of the way people lived in our day, we are reminded to find contentment in our marriage. Today we find people changing spouses the way they change clothes. We are not to commit sexual immorality or adultery. God says He will punish those who are sexually immoral and adulterers.
We don't seek extra-marital affairs, we don't say, oops, it just happened.

It's finding contentment and joy, along with power, strength and compassion in your marriage.

Finally, the writer starts out verse 5 by saying

Hebrews 13:5
Let your conversation be without covetousness;

In other words, keep your life free from the love of money, and be content with what you have

Understand that money, in and of itself is not bad. It's actually a good, if not great thing!! Money isn't bad! But the love of money can be terribly destructive. We end up trying to accumulate as much as we can.
Get as much as you can and can as much as you can get. That is the way of today. We want more and more and more. We're never satisfied with what we have. Someone else has more, so we want more.

The world doesn't understand what a Christ followers' contentment and peace is about. They see it, and they want it, but that is not tangible. The world sees what you wear, they see your car, your home, your electronics and toys. That's how they judge you.

So, we focus on those things which will spoil, fade and perish. We should work hard to get ahead. We should save money. But we should not hoard our money. We should not hoard things. Its not about how much we can get, but how much we can give.

The love of money and worldly possessions is what leads to our sinfulness. So, we keep our money hidden. We store away our treasures in bags that have holes. Then when it comes time to go home, we find that we have nothing. Jesus told us:

Luke 12:16-34

And he spake a parable unto them, saying, The ground of a certain rich man brought forth plentifully: And he thought within himself, saying, What shall I do, because I have no room where to bestow my fruits? And he said, This will I do: I will pull down my barns, and build greater; and there will I bestow all my fruits and my goods. And I will say to my soul, Soul, thou hast much goods laid up for many years; take thine ease, eat, drink, and be merry. But God said unto him, Thou fool, this night thy soul shall be required of thee: then whose shall those things be, which thou hast provided? So is he that layeth up treasure for himself, and is not rich toward God. And he said unto his disciples, Therefore I say unto you, Take no thought for your life, what ye shall eat; neither for the body, what ye shall put on.

The life is more than meat, and the body is more than raiment. Consider the ravens: for they neither sow nor reap; which neither have storehouse nor barn; and God feedeth them: how much more are ye better than the fowls? And which of you with taking thought can add to his stature one cubit? If ye then be not able to do that thing which is least, why take ye thought for the rest? Consider the lilies how they grow: they toil not, they spin not; and yet I say unto you, that Solomon in all his glory was not arrayed like one of these. If then God so clothe the grass, which is to day in the field, and to morrow is cast into the oven; how much more will he clothe you, O ye of little faith? And seek not ye what ye shall eat, or what ye shall drink, neither be ye of doubtful mind.

For all these things do the nations of the world seek after:
and your Father knoweth that ye have need of these things.
But rather seek ye the kingdom of God; and all these
things shall be added unto you. Fear not, little flock; for it
is your Father's good pleasure to give you the kingdom.
Sell that ye have, and give alms; provide yourselves bags
which wax not old, a treasure in the heavens that faileth
not, where no thief approacheth, neither moth corrupteth.
For where your treasure is, there will your heart be also.

So many churches today have become hoarders and the
people of the church have followed suit.
We don't give to charities,
We don't give to missionaries,
We don't give to the poor,
We don't give to those in need.
Yet, we spend on things which we really don't need
because it gives us a quick fix. We look at our shiny new
toy and feel good about ourselves, then someone else gets
a newer and better one and that good feeling fades away.
So, the writer of Hebrews is reminding us to be content.

I do not think that any of us would bow down to an idol.
Remember, our money and possessions are a gift from
God. And these can certainly become our gods if we are
not careful. It has been said, first we make the god and
then the god begins making us. That is exactly what
happens with money and possessions if we are not careful.

With all of this in mind the writer leads us to our
conclusion, which is exactly where we started. We are to
be people who are filled with compassion and
contentment. We can do that because we have this
amazing promise from God

Hebrews 13:5
I will never leave thee, nor forsake thee.

God's promise is very clear He will never, never leave you AND He will never, never forsake you!! So, does that mean God has never forsaken anyone who belonged to Him? Anyone who believed in Him, trusted in Him, loved Him?

Actually, that answer is YES! There was a person who was forsaken by God.

We are told in the Scriptures that the crowds mocked Jesus while He was on the cross.
Matthew 27:46
And about the ninth hour Jesus cried out with a loud voice, saying, "Eloi, Eloi, lema sabachthani?" that is, "My God, my God, why have you forsaken me?"

Jesus was quoting the first words of Psalm 22. In this unique and strange miracle, Jesus was crying out in anguish because of the separation He now experienced from His Heavenly Father.

It was the first time He felt separated from His Father. This is the only time Jesus did not address God as the Father.

Why? Because the Son had taken sin upon Himself, and the Father could not be part of that and had to turn away from Him. For a time, between about 3 pm to 6 pm, there was separation between the Son and the Father.

The sin of the world, your sins and mine, the sins of humanity were thrust upon Jesus during this time. The words of Paul state it well in 2 Corinthians 5

2 Corinthians 5:21
For our sake God made Him to be sin who knew no sin, so that in Him we might become the righteousness of God.

Our sinfulness entering His beaten body. Jesus died as a substitute sacrifice for the sins of the world. God literally took our sin and shame and abandonment upon Himself so that we would not have to.

Jesus was forsaken so that we would never ever never have to be forsaken.

And because of that we can confidently say,

Hebrews 13:6
So that we may boldly say, The Lord is my helper, and I will not fear what man shall do unto me.

Chapter 3
A Church Ready

We have all heard the saying "Blessed by the best."
Who is the best? Of course, if you are a Chrisitan we
know that the best is Jesus Christ Himself. Ther is no one
like Jesus. He is better than anything this world has to
offer. He is the greatest of the greatest. Not just for what
He does for us in bringing us salvation, but for His great
love for us. As a Christian, someone who has followed the
Lord's plan of salvation, we have nothing to fear. Not
even in death. There is nothing to fear. David says "Yea
though I walk through the valley of the shadow of death, I
will fear no evil." There is nothing to fear even in death
once we have followed God's plan of salvation. Paul had
this assurance. When he is writing his last letter to his son
in the faith Timothy, he is encouraging him not to worry,
not even in death. Let's look at 2nd Timothy 4:6-8.

2nd Timothy 4:6-8
For I am now ready to be offered, and the time of my
departure is at hand. I have fought a good fight, I have
finished my course, I have kept the faith: Henceforth there
is laid up for me a crown of righteousness, which the Lord,
the righteous judge, shall give me at that day: and not to
me only, but unto all them also that love his appearing.

This is Paul's swan song. Paul knows his time is almost
finished.
Death is something we will all have to face someday
unless the Lord Jesus comes back first.

30 years some of the people you know are not going to be
here.
60 years even less of the people you know will be here.
100 years none of us will be here.

When we think of death we think of friends and family.
We think of Funeral homes and flowers,
We think of Dying and crying,
We think of Graves and coffins,
But that is not the case for those that have followed Jesus
Christ plan of salvation.
Here in this scripture Paul gives us another idea of death
for those that have truly been saved.

Notice 3 things Paul mentions.
His departure, in verse 6
His declaration, in verse 7
And his destination, in verse 8.

First Paul says my departure is at hand.

2nd Timothy 4:6
For I am now ready to be offered, and the time of my
departure is at hand.

This word departure has so many different meanings.
For the sailor it means to untie the ship from the dock and
begin sailing.
No longer fastened to the dock No longer held back, but
finally cut loose.

Have you ever watched a ship sail out into the horizon?
Eventually it disappears. But just because you cannot see
it any more does not mean it has quit sailing. When it
leaves the harbor here there is a goodbye, when it arrives
at the next harbor, on the other side there is a hello.
Goodbye here is hello there for those who have trusted in
God's plan of salvation.

There was an old song I used to hear the folks sing in the church.
Tis the old ship of Zion
Tis the old ship of Zion
Tis the old ship of Zion
Get on board get on board

It has landed many a thousand
It has landed many a thousand
It has landed many a thousand
Get on board get on board

Aint no danger in the water
Aint no danger in the water
Aint no danger in the water
Get on board get on board

But the last verse is the best verse.

It has Jesus as its captain.
It has Jesus as its captain.
It has Jesus as its captain.
Get on board get on board

For those that have followed God's plan of salvation there is a day coming when that old ship of Zion is going to be passing by. Jesus is going to call get on board and it will be on that day that we will sail off into the sunset with Jesus as our guild.

Paul says my departure is at hand.

In Military terms it means to take down the tents.

It means to fold up the cots and roll up the sleeping bags. It means it is time to move to a new camp. It doesn't mean that the captain has left us. It means that we will no longer be staying in this camp.

That is what death is for those that have followed through with God's plan of salvation. As a true follower of Jesus Christ we are on a journey.

This is not our home child of God. We can't be satisfied here. We are looking for a home, we are looking for a city whose builder and maker is God.

One of these days we are moving camp sites. Why?
Will it be because we song in the choir?
Will it be because we gave money to the church?
Will it be because we were good to people?
No because we followed God's plan of salvation. Jesus is going to call us to a different camp where our traveling and battling days will be over.
Not only is the word departure a military term and a sailor's term, but it is an agricultural term.

In the agricultural world the word departure is that time of day when you leave the field. It is when the famer leads the mule or horse back home, back to the barn. It was when the plowing was finished. It is when the yoke was taken off of the animal and the animal was given rest for the night. The burdens are lifted. There are no more struggles. No more challenges. The work is over.

For those who have put their trust in Jesus Christ and followed His plan of salvation, death will be that time when the yoke is taken off of you. It will be when the burdens of this life are lifted.

Matthew 11:28-30
Come unto me, all ye that labour and are heavy laden, and I will give you rest. Take my yoke upon you, and learn of me; for I am meek and lowly in heart: and ye shall find rest unto your souls. For my yoke is easy, and my burden is light.

I want you to realize that you cannot wait until you leave here to make your departure plans. The plans must be made before you leave here otherwise it will be too late. Paul made his plans before he left. He put everything in order before leaving earth.

Notice not only Paul's departure, but Paul's declaration. Verse 7

2nd Timothy 4:7
I have fought a good fight, I have finished my course, I have kept the faith:

First of all, Paul says I have fought a good fight. The Christian life is a fight to the end. You have to be a fighter to be a follower. Our fight is not with our hands. Our fight is not with our feet. The greatest fight we can make against the enemy is on our knees.

Romans 8:31
What shall we then say to these things? If God be for us, who can be against us?

Isaiah 54:17
No weapon that is formed against thee shall prosper; and
every tongue that shall rise against thee in judgment thou
shalt condemn. This is the heritage of the servants of the
Lord, and their righteousness is of me, saith the Lord.

Our fighting is not with our hands
Our fighting is not with our intellect
Our fighting is not with our knowledge or our wisdom

The greatest fighting, we can do is on our knees. The
battle is not ours; the battle belongs to the Lord.

2nd Timothy 1:7
For God hath not given us the spirit of fear; but of power,
and of love, and of a sound mind.

I have heard it said when a saint of God is battling cancer
or if a saint of God is battling leukemia or AIDS, I have
heard it said that when they die they lost their battle with
their sickness. He lost his battle with cancer. She lost her
battle with leukemia. I want you to realize that they did
not loose their battle. God can use what ever method He
chooses to take us home, as a saint of God.

For some He may use sickness.
For others He may use an accident.
For others He may use may use old age.

Some would say that Covid has taken the life of many of
the fighting saints. I want us to realize that it is not a
sickness that takes out a fighting saint of God.

It is not an accident that take out a fighting saint of God. It is not a war or a battle that defeats the fighting saint of God, that takes them home. Realize this, it was God's means of salvation that brought them into His presence.

If the person died with cancer after fighting hard and serving the Lord, it was not the cancer that defeated them. The cancer was just God's transportation method to bring them into His Presence.

It was not leukemia that killed a fighting saint of God. The Lord used that illness to get them into His Presence.

God can use whatever He likes to bring a saint of God into His presence

For Elijah it was horses of fire and a chariot of fire.
For Enoch it was a walk.
For Moses He used old age.

The key to fighting the Chrisitan life is not to give up.

The devil will try to get you to give up. The devil says just let go.

In the storm, just let go.
If there is strife in your house the enemy says, just turn loose.
If there is sadness and sorrow the enemy says let go.
If there is sickness and suffering the enemy says turn loose of the grip you have on the Lord.

In trails and temptations, just let go

But then there is Jesus on the other side saying, just hold on.
Just hold on a little longer daughter,
Just hold on a little longer son
You are almost there, you can do it, just hold on.
You are too near the end now, just hold on

The old song goes,

Precious Lord take my hand, lead me on, let me stand
I am tired, I am weak, I am worn.
Through the storm, through the night
Lead me on to the night
Take my hand, precious Lord and lead me home.

Someday it is going to be worth it.
Death is not the end. Death is just the beginning for those who have truly trusted in Jesus Christ and His plan of salvation.

Paul says I have fought a good fight,
He says I have finished my course. He says I have finished my race.
God has a plan for each of us.

Jeremiah 29:11
For I know the thoughts that I think toward you, saith the Lord, thoughts of peace, and not of evil, to give you an expected end.

Hebrews 12:1

Wherefore seeing we also are compassed about with so great a cloud of witnesses, let us lay aside every weight, and the sin which doth so easily beset us, and let us run with patience the race that is set before us,

We have all been given a race to run. When our race is finished there is no need to stay on the field any longer. When a ball game is over, no one sets around waiting.

When a race is over, no one sets around waiting. They go home. God has a race for each of us. We don't know the length of the race. We don't know when it will be finished. The Lord has a start time for each of us and He has an end time for each of us. Paul says I have fought a good fight. I have finished my course.

Next, Paul says I have kept the faith. I have been faithful to the end. I kept hanging on to Jesus. I didn't let go.
When things got slippery, I got a tighter hold.
When things got stormy, I just moved closer to the Lord.
The Bible says, He that endures to the end, shall be saved.

We have seen Paul's departure,
We have seen Paul's declaration,
Let's look at Paul's destination.

2nd Timothy 4;8
Henceforth there is laid up for me a crown of righteousness, which the Lord, the righteous judge, shall give me at that day: and not to me only, but unto all them also that love his appearing.

Death for the Christian is a place of revelation:

When we close our eyes here, the next face we will see is the blessed face of our Lord Jesus Christ.

Psalm 116:15
Precious in the sight of the Lord is the death of His saints.

There is an old poem that gives us an idea of what death is going to be like for the true Christian.

Face to face with Christ my Savior,
Face to face--what will it be
When with rapture I behold Him,
Jesus Christ who died for me?

Face to face I shall behold Him,
Far beyond the starry sky;
Face to face in all His glory,
I shall see Him by and by!

Only faintly now I see Him
With the darkened veil between,
But a blessed day is coming
When His glory shall be seen.

What rejoicing in His presence,
When are banished grief and pain;
When the crooked ways are straightened
And the dark things shall be plain.

Face to face--oh, blissful moment!
Face to face--to see and know;
Face to face with my Redeemer,
Jesus Christ who loves me so.

It's a place of revelation

2ndly it is a place of reward.
Paul says I will have a crown, a mansion, I will have a ring, I will be freed from sin and temptation. I will be freed from sickness and grief.

There will be golden streets, there will be life in everything with no death at all. There will be beauty beyond what our mind can comprehend. But the greatest thing about heaven. What will truly make heaven, heaven, is that Jesus will be there. There is no greater place to be than in the Lord's presence. That is the heart of every true Christian. Just wanting to be with their Savior. Heaven will be heaven, all because Jesus is there.

It will be a place of revelation.
It will be a place of reward,
It will be a place of reckoning.

Paul called Jesus the righteous judge.

The Lord has given us His plan of salvation. It is not man's plan, it is not a Baptist plan or a Pentecostal plan, it is God's plan.

What is God's plan?

Acts 2:38
Then Peter said unto them, Repent, and be baptized every one of you in the name of Jesus Christ for the remission of sins, and ye shall receive the gift of the Holy Ghost.

The first thing the Bible says it that we must repent, not repeat.
Some say just come forward and say this pray and you will be saved. The Bible never said that. The Bible says to repent. It means turning with a godly sorrow.

Secondly, be baptized every one of you in the name of Jesus Christ for the remission of sins

Mark 16:16
He that believeth and is baptized shall be saved; but he that believeth not shall be damned.

1st Peter 3:21
whereunto even baptism doth also now save u

The Bible says that baptism is required for salvation. And notice not only is baptism required, but the way is required.

1. Baptism, completely submerged
2. In Jesus Name.
        Acts 2 the Jews are baptized in Jesus Name
        Acts 8 the Samaritans are baptized in Jesus name
        Acts 10 the Gentiles are baptized in Jesus Name
        Acts 19 those that had been baptized in John's
baptism were rebaptized in Jesus Name.

If you could have been baptized anyway the Lord would have said it. But He told us how. But what about Matthew 28?

Matthew 28:19

Go ye therefore, and teach all nations, baptizing them in the name of the Father, and of the Son, and of the Holy Ghost:

These are titles. Realize there are not 3 Gods in heaven. When the question was asked of Jesus what is the greatest commandment. Jesus said in Mark 12:28-29

Mark 12:28-29
And one of the scribes came, and having heard them reasoning together, and perceiving that he had answered them well, asked him, Which is the first commandment of all? And Jesus answered him, The first of all the commandments is, Hear, O Israel; The Lord our God is one Lord:

There is One God in heaven. His Name Jesus.

What is God's plan of salvation?

1. Repent
2. Be baptized in the Name of Jesus
3. Receive the Holy Ghost
Acts 2:38
Then Peter said unto them, Repent, and be baptized every one of you in the name of Jesus Christ for the remission of sins, and ye shall receive the gift of the Holy Ghost.

If you will do the repenting, and get baptized in Jesus Name, God will do His part.

One day we all will have to give an account.

Did we follow God's plan of salvation?

Were we faithful to the end?

I remember hearing a story of a little boy that was dying with cancer. His mom and dad knew that it would not be much longer. The little boy was laying in his bed with his mother sitting beside him. He looked at her and asked this question.

"Mama will it hurt?" the boy said.

"Will what hurt his mama asked?"

"When I die," the little boy said.

The mother was choked up trying to fight back the tears, wondering how she might answer her son's question. Finally, after a few moments of silence the Lord gave her the words.

The mother said, "Son, do you remember how you used to fall asleep on the couch downstairs in front of the tv. You would fall asleep watching tv, but the next morning when you woke up, you were not on the couch anymore but in your room."

"Yes mama," the boy said.

"Have you ever wondered how you got to your room? I mean you fell asleep on the couch, but woke up in your room," the mother said.

"Yes," said the boy.

"Let me tell you what happens," said mother, "Your father comes downstairs and finds you sleeping on the couch and then with his big strong arms he picks you up and takes you to your room and lays you down in your bed. When you wake up there you are safe and secure in your bed. That is what death is going to be like Son," said his mama. "When you die, you are going to close your eyes and fall asleep, just like you do on the couch, and Jesus with His Big strong arms is going to come and pick you up and carry you to heave where you will be with Him forever."

That is what death is for those that have followed God's plan of salvation. How about you? Have you repented, been baptized in the Name of Jesus for the remission of sins and received the Holy Ghost? If not then you can start your journey today. Be ready for your departure. Jesus is calling you today.

Chapter 4
A Church Focused

Hebrews 12:1-5
Wherefore seeing we also are compassed about with so
great a cloud of witnesses, let us lay aside every weight,
and the sin which doth so easily beset us, and let us run
with patience the race that is set before us, looking unto
Jesus the author and finisher of our faith; who for the joy
that was set before him endured the cross, despising the
shame, and is set down at the right hand of the throne of
God. For consider him that endured such contradiction of
sinners against himself, lest ye be wearied and faint in
your minds. Ye have not yet resisted unto blood, striving
against sin. And ye have forgotten the exhortation which
speaketh unto you as unto children, My son, despise not
thou the chastening of the Lord, nor faint when thou art
rebuked of him:

Have you ever exercised wearing weights? It sounds kind
of strange, but people do this. In fact, I have known people
who wear weighted vest to workout. These vest weigh 20
pounds. On the one hand, it may not sound that bad, but do
20 pushups wearing a 20-pound vest, and after a few
minutes it begins to feel like more than 20 pounds.

If you've been jogging, maybe you wore ankle weights to
force your legs to work harder. Throw a medicine ball in
the air a few times, then throw a basketball in the air and it
feels lighter than it normally does.

This is what I want us to look at today, but it's not to hold
onto the weights, it's to get rid of the weights. The goal is
to lighten the load, not make it heavier and heavier and
harder and more difficult as we move down the road. So,

that's what we're looking at today. And as we move along, I'll talk about some of the different weights we hold onto which truly weigh us down. And the one main weight we cling to according to Hebrews 12.

Let's look again at the first verses of Hebrews 12

Hebrews 12:1-3
Wherefore seeing we also are compassed about with so great a cloud of witnesses, let us lay aside every weight, and the sin which doth so easily beset us, and let us run with patience the race that is set before us, Looking unto Jesus the author and finisher of our faith; who for the joy that was set before him endured the cross, despising the shame, and is set down at the right hand of the throne of God. For consider him that endured such contradiction of sinners against himself, lest ye be wearied and faint in your minds.

Here the writer told us we're surrounded by this great cloud of witnesses. These witnesses are more than your loved ones who are in heaven, who are your cheerleaders. These are the saints of the OT. People like Moses, Aaron, Abraham, Sarah, Rahab, Jacob, Jeremiah, Hosea, Deborah and 1,000's of faithful servants for God.

They're encouraging and cheering you on through the difficulties of life. The beauty and the power is the fact that not one of these Bible characters were perfect. They all had faults, they all needed Jesus, YET none of them ever attained the glory of meeting Jesus in this world yet they never gave up on their faith, they still trusted, believed, and had faith that the God who called them was not going to abandon them. That's why they're in the Hall of Fame of Faith!

The 3rd part of verse 1 tells us we should run with endurance the race which God has set out before us. Remember the Greek word for race is our English word AGONY. It means conflict and struggle. It means that race which is life is going to be filled with difficulties and struggles. God never promised us that life would be clean and easy. It can be dirty and difficult. Yet, God calls us to stay on the path He's set out for us.

And we run that race with endurance. We don't give up, we don't give in, we don't say this hurts, so it must not be God's will. It might not be . . . but it may also be part of God's plan. Remember so many of those in the stands cheering you on lived lives filled with struggle, pain and suffering. We're no different than these saints. Even in our own family and among our own friends we find so many of our beloved saints that have struggled or are struggling, we see the concerns, we see the hurt . . . YET at the very same time, we see the hope, the grace the mercy and the power of the risen Christ in your eyes and hearts. And that my friends gives us tremendous hope!!

So, I want to move into the middle of verse 1, what we would call verse 1b. Let's read the passage

Hebrews 12:1
Therefore, since we are surrounded by so great a cloud of witnesses,

let us also lay aside every weight, and sin which clings so closely, and let us run with endurance the race that is set before us,

OK, so let's focus on what the writer means when he tells us

let us also lay aside every weight, and sin which clings so closely,

Remember the writer of Hebrews is using athletic imagery. In this athletic imagery, he's talking about weights like I spoke about at the beginning of this message. When we compete, we need to discard those weights so that we can fully compete.

It's important to understand a couple of definitions. The first comes in the word WEIGHT - it means a burden or something which weighs you down. That kind of makes sense. But the next word doesn't seem to make as much sense. It's the PHRASE we have in the ESV - CLINGS SO CLOSELY. In the KJV it's EASILY ENSNARES. And the NIV states EASILY ENTANGLES.

So, what does that really mean? Literally - that phrase means - - - a serious hindrance that "encircles" (hampers) someone who desperately needs to advance.

If you have ever watched American football, you will see someone who gets the ball and the other team tries to take the man with the ball down. They are hanging onto him and trying to pull at him, they are trying to hinder him and stop him from finishing his race. That is the kind of picture we get.

You cannot run the long distance race if you are always impeded by any kind of weight that holds you back. It becomes exhausting. You have to get rid of those things which weigh you down. You may train in ankle weights, but when you come to the track meet, you don't have your weights on. You run with nothing hindering your progress.

Can you imagine walking up to the starting line and wearing your ankle weights? The coach yells out "You forgot to take off your ankle weights!" And you say, "No! I've grown accustomed to them. I like them. I'm going to run with them today!" No one in their right mind would run with weights!

You wouldn't do that . . . would you? Of course, I know what you're going to say . . . NO WAY!! I would never do that. Yet we do!

Why is it so many of us are carrying in bulging backpacks of bitterness? You plop them down in the seat beside you. Some of you were carrying vests filled with anger. Your bag was checked at the door, but you'll pick it up on the way out. Some of you were bent over from so many years of carrying around a big old trunk full of all kinds of weight that's holding you back as a Christian. It's so heavy it wouldn't even fit between the pews. When you sat down you had to sit on the end and plop it down in the aisle.

Some of us are carrying around heavy bags of resentment, there's selfishness, addictions, arrogance, self-loathing, idolatry, greed, critical spirit . . . .and that list can go on and on and on.

We carry those sins with us. We find a few minutes of relief in worship . . . as long as we can put that critical spirit away, then we grab our struggles as we walk out the door. Ever feel that way? I know I've been there too many times.

Our aisles and pews are filled with handbags and backpacks and trunks of all kinds of weights that spiritual athletes, you and I. We bring it in every time the doors of the church open. We act like all is well. We act as if there are no problems. Why do we do that? We can't succeed in the Christian life that way. We must do as the Bible tells us . . . . to LAY ASIDE EVERY WEIGHT / BURDEN. This means to "lay aside or renounce" anything that would hinder you.

In the first century, when runners came to the Olympic Games, they would wear long, flowing, colorful robes. And at the last minute, before the race began, they would take them off. In fact, many runners in that time ran naked. They didn't want to be impeded in any way in their race.

The writer of Hebrews tells us we must discard not only the weights, but our sin as well. While I believe we carry a lot of sin into church - - and there's really no better place to bring our sin, but we can't take it back when we leave. I believe the author is not just talking about all of our sins, but he's more specifically telling us to remove the weights of the sin which so easily grabs ahold of us and that sin is faithlessness, shame guilt and discouragement.

Remember, he's just listed great men and women who by faith won the victory. That's the reference here; the sin that so easily entangles is the lack of faith. Many times, if we do lay off the sin we still walk in the shame and guilt of it. These become weights in our Christian life.

Our lives in Christ begins with faith in Jesus. It's when we proclaim Jesus is Lord and Savior. We repent of our sins and are baptized in the Name of Jesus, receiving the promised gift of the Holy Ghost. But it doesn't stop there. We must live every day by faith. In fact, at the end of chapter 10 leading into 11, the author quoted Habakkuk 2:4, "The just shall live by faith." That's the focus leading up to this passage.

But some of us don't like to live by faith; we want to live by sight. We want to get the calculator out and figure out how everything works. It's not easy to live by faith. Most of us don't like that idea. I don't! I want to know what's going to happen. It goes against our nature. Yet, we are called to live by faith.

So, the author tells us if we can lay aside every weight which holds us back, then we can run with endurance the race which has been set before us. You see that little phrase "with endurance?" The focus is on endurance. Life is not a speed event, it's an endurance super marathon event. It is not about who can finish first, it is about enduring until the end.

Have you ever noticed when you drive a long distance, sometimes you don't really remember turning on your street or getting off the highway at the right exit? Has that ever happened to you? I know it has to me. It's like I was day dreaming or thinking about 101 other things than driving. That's not how we are supposed to approach this race.

As we're running this race, the writer tells us - we run - -

Hebrews 12:2
looking to Jesus, the (author and finisher) <u>founder and perfecter of our faith,</u>

While we have all these witnesses, these great saints cheering and encouraging us, and we have our family and church family encouraging us . . . ultimately, we are to look only at Jesus.

Next
Have you ever watched someone run backwards and they don't run in a straight line? Or they do backstroke and have no idea where in the pool they are? That's not how we run the race of life.

You see, we must be looking at Jesus. He's the focus of our attention. Jesus will never let us down. If you look at others, somehow, they'll let you down, we can become discouraged, but when we fix our eyes upon Jesus, He promises not to abandon you, but to be with you throughout your entire journey.

Have you ever been frustrated with someone because they seem to have blinders on? They can only see one thing; they don't see the big picture. In a strange way that's what the word LOOKING means. The implication is that we fix our eyes on Jesus and in a sense, we wear blinders so that all other distractions are moved out of our way. Isn't that true in life? We allow so many distractions get in our way. Wasn't that the problem Martha was having with Mary? Our focus must be on Jesus and only Jesus. If our focus is not on Jesus, then we are going to lose our way and we will get way off track.

So, I am to fix my eyes on Jesus, the author, the first, the pioneer of my faith. The One who perfects our faith - - who for the joy that was set before Him endured the cross,

Why am I to look at Jesus? He also ran the spiritual marathon. He came into this world in the incarnation. He took on human flesh. He became what we are. He remained who He is — God — but He became who we are — man: Jesus became the God-man. And He lived in our world, living a sinless life. He is the One we are to look towards.

Notice the Bible says, "for the joy set before Him endured the cross." It's not easy to see joy and cross in the same sentence. It's almost like an oxymoron.

I believe this is a reference to the completion of God's will for Jesus' life, knowing that God's will was that His Son would suffer and die for our sins. So, Jesus did this with joy as the obedient Son of the Father. It wasn't fun, it was painful and terrible suffering, but His closeness to the Father is what brought Jesus through this. And the fact that He was reconciling you and me to the Father brought Jesus joy.

Jesus fulfilled the will of the Father. But He also knew the cross was not going to be the end of the story. He knew there was a resurrection and an ascension to come as well. He knew without a doubt what was coming. So Jesus endured the cross - -

despising the shame, and is seated at the right hand of the throne of God.

Jesus is enthroned there. As Hebrews 6:19-20 reminds us ~

Hebrews 6:19-20
Which hope we have as an anchor of the soul, both sure and stedfast, and which entereth into that within the veil; Whither the forerunner is for us entered, even Jesus, made an high priest for ever after the order of Melchisedec.

Jesus is the anchor for my soul, He has destroyed the bonds that satan has over me. He has destroyed what weighs me down. Now I use Jesus as my anchor, so that I will not move in the wrong direction. He is my north star, my spiritual compass. Whatever phrase you want to use, that's Jesus. He endured the Cross; He despised the shame; He suffered all of that! And then He sat down at the right hand of the throne of God. Nothing can ever remove Him, because He endured for us.
Finally, verse 3 tells us ~

Hebrews 12:3
Least ye be weary and faint in your minds

We've really had applications throughout this passage. We are to fix our eyes on Jesus. We are to take those weights off, get rid of the sin which so easily entangles us, with endurance we are to run the race.

We are to consider JESUS - who endured. Did you notice the word endurance is in all 3 verses. This is part of our focus. Because Jesus has endured, " *For consider him that endured such contradiction of sinners against himself,*" This is everything Jesus went through.

The rejection, the temptation, the disavowal by His family, desertion, the lies, the betrayal, the misunderstanding, the beating, the mocking, the shouts, the spitting, the nails! Yet, Jesus endured!

When we consider all that Jesus went through . . . what He went through for you and me . . . it should encourage and strengthen us to continue to run with endurance that race which God has set before us . . . because Jesus also endured. He knows what it's like to be in your shoes.

In the end we do not grow weary or fainthearted because Jesus has already paid the price for you and I.

Therefore, the author of Hebrews says,

Hebrews 12:1-2
Wherefore seeing we also are compassed about with so great a cloud of witnesses, let us lay aside every weight, and the sin which doth so easily beset us, and let us run with patience the race that is set before us, Looking unto Jesus the author and finisher of our faith; who for the joy that was set before him endured the cross, despising the shame, and is set down at the right hand of the throne of God. For consider him (focus on Him, meditate on Him, live the rest of your life looking at Him) *that endured such*

contradiction of sinners against himself, (Why?) *lest ye be wearied and faint in your minds.*

Amen!!!

Made in the USA
Middletown, DE
01 March 2023